Enneagram:

The #1 Made Easy Guide to the 9 Types of Personalities. Grow Your Self-Awareness, Evolve Your Personality, and Build Healthy Relationships. Find the Strength for Life's Changes and Challenges.

by

Tina Madison

The following eBook is reproduced below with the goal of providing information that is as accurate and reliable as possible. Regardless, purchasing this eBook can be seen as consent to the fact that both the publisher and the author of this book are in no way experts on the topics discussed within and that any recommendations or suggestions that are made herein are for entertainment purposes only. Professionals should be consulted as needed prior to undertaking any of the action endorsed herein.

This declaration is deemed fair and valid by both the American Bar Association and the Committee of Publishers Association and is legally binding throughout the United States.

Furthermore, the transmission, duplication or reproduction of any of the following work including specific information will be considered an illegal act irrespective of if it is done electronically or in print. This extends to creating a secondary or tertiary copy of the work or a recorded copy and is only allowed with an expressed written consent from the Publisher. All additional right reserved.

The information in the following pages is broadly considered to be a truthful and accurate account of facts, and as such any inattention, use or misuse of the information in question by the reader will render any resulting actions solely under their purview. There are no scenarios in which the publisher or the original author of this work can be in any fashion deemed liable for any hardship or damages that may befall them after undertaking information described herein.

Additionally, the information in the following pages is intended only for informational purposes and should thus be thought of as universal. As befitting its nature, it is presented without assurance regarding its prolonged validity or interim quality. Trademarks that are mentioned are done without written consent and can in no way be considered an endorsement from the trademark holder.

Introduction

The Enneagram is an ancient tool used to identify personality types in people. It recognizes nine different personality types and twenty-seven subtypes. Each of these is dedicated to helping people understand themselves on a deeper level, allowing them to maximize their self-expression, deepen their relationships, and experience their best life possible.

In the following pages, you are going to be introduced to this ancient tool and how it works. You will also discover which type you are and learn about the subtypes related to your personality type. This will give you a greater understanding of who you are and why you are the way you are.

Through this journey, you are going to be introduced to a level of self-awareness that will change your life. This self-awareness will bring you the ability to recognize why you are the way you are, highlight blind spots that you may not recognize in yourself, and discover and explore ways that you can choose to act in a different and more empowering and positive way. In doing so, you will discover how you can balance your personality type and experience a positive self - expression in life, relationships, and career.

If you are ready to discover the Enneagram personality test and what it can do for you, it's time to get started! Please, take your time, allow yourself to absorb the information that is within this book, and of course, enjoy!

Part 1: Understanding the Enneagram

Chapter 1: What Is the Enneagram?

The Enneagram is a tool that is used by many as a means to motivate, inspire, and guide personal and collective transformation.

The word itself stems from two Greek words: ennea, which means "nine," and grammos, which means "a written symbol." This refers to the nine points on the symbol that are relevant to the nine different types found on the Enneagram.

Each of the nine types featured on the Enneagram is personalized with their own unique thinking patterns, feelings, and actions that stem from both inner motivation and outer worldview.

Using the Enneagram, personal development can be accomplished using a universal language that does not segregate individuals based on their gender, nationality, religion, or culture. It realizes that we are all unique, but also understands that we all share common experiences which therefore contribute to our ability to be classified into the nine different types.

It is important to understand that, in discovering which type you are classified into based on your Enneagram test results, you are not boxing yourself in a specific personality type that does not allow room for growth. Instead, you are gaining insight into the box from which you view the world, and learning how this box may be presently limiting you, and what you can do to broaden your life experiences. When you become consciously aware of the limitations that you have placed on yourself based on your Enneagram type, you can then begin to take inspired action that aligns with your type to gently release these limits and begin experiencing your best life possible.

To summarize, the Enneagram is a written symbol that features nine different personality types. Upon finding which type you are, you can also learn how to express yourself, broaden your self-awareness, evolve your personality, build stronger and healthier relationships, and overcome the many trials and tribulations that we face in life.

Chapter 2: Your Identity

As humans, at one point or another in our lives, we tend to dwell on this question: "Who am I?"

It is this very question that compels us to begin searching for the meaning of life and the meaning of ourselves. We desire to fill our lives with meaning and purpose so that we can experience fulfillment in our lifetime.

Something we tend to do, as human beings, is try to identify ourselves as fragments of our whole self. As a result of our insecurities and fears, we fabricate and share the belief that we are only the best parts of ourselves. What results is that we end up dishonoring massive realities within who we are. This is because we do not want to admit that there are aspects of ourselves that we don't like, so instead, we simply cut them out. We then do the same thing when introducing ourselves to others, as well. We will introduce ourselves and who we are by ignoring the aspects that bring us fear, shame, guilt, or otherwise unhappy feelings.

We believe that the things we do make us who we are when in reality, that is not the truth. We are not what we do, or what we have done. We are a human *being*. No, a human *doing*. However, through the process of societal conditioning that we have received throughout our lives, we have been led to believe that we are only as good as the things we do. If we do things that are considered to be bad or somehow unwanted, unappreciated, or unaccepted by society, we believe we *are* bad. We tend to want to hide these aspects of ourselves to prevent other people from thinking we are a bad person. Similarly, when we do things that are deemed acceptable, admirable, and seen as a good thing to society, we believe we *are* good. We tend to highlight and amplify our focus on these aspects as an opportunity to increase our value and self-worth.

The reality is that nothing you do actually affects who you are. This is just something that you have been conditioned to believe. Who you *are* is not measured by something you do. It is measured by who you are as a being.

The process of coming home to your identity means shedding the belief that anything you do has an impact on who you are. What you do is an important aspect of your life, certainly, but it has absolutely zero impact on who you truly are. Staying stuck in this belief will only keep you away from your true self longer.

Coming back to yourself means that you shed away these beliefs and you get into the true facts of who you are. This is not measured by good or bad. It is only measured by what *is*. It is your beingness. It is the true reality of who you are at your core, underneath the things that you do. Getting back into the core reality of who you are means that you open up the doors for yourself to become who you truly are once more. When we live out of alignment with this reality, we tend to act and behave in ways that are not aligned with the truth, the whole unfragmented truth, of who we are. When we live in alignment with this core being, we act and behave in ways that are empowered, aligned, and accurate to who we are.

Chapter 3: Your Journey

When you embark on your journey with the Enneagram, you are going to find yourself exposed to many opportunities to come home to yourself, grow, and become more aligned with who you truly are. You can use the Enneagram to gain a greater sense of your identity, understand your tendencies and patterns, and use this knowledge to live in alignment with your greatest life, and your whole self.

The journey with the Enneagram will start by taking an Enneagram test. This test will determine which type you are on the Enneagram. You will also learn about subtypes. This information will support you greatly in the process of understanding who you are, what your tendencies are, and why. As a result of having a reason or meaning behind these tendencies, you will then be able to understand yourself with a greater sense of self-awareness. This means that you can identify these processes and tendencies in advance, understand why they happen, and consciously choose to behave differently in a way that still aligns with who you are as a person. You are going to learn about all of the growth opportunities that exist for you, how you can become your best self, and the importance of expressing yourself in alignment with your truth.

The journey may be somewhat shocking or emotional, as you are drawn to look at the fragments of yourself that you may have abandoned throughout the years. However, once you shine a light on these aspects, you can find ways to support yourself in growth going forward. This means that you can begin to reintegrate these parts of yourself and live your life feeling whole, as opposed to consistently trying to hide these aspects of you that are part of your true reality and beingness.

If you are ready to begin, head into part two where you can take the Enneagram test.

Part 2: The Test

Chapter 4: Enneagram Test Instructions

In the Enneagram test in Chapter 5, you are going to be shown a table. This table will include numbers, statements, and then columns for the letters A, B, C, D, E, F, G, H, and I.

Each number will have two statements next to it. You will notice that next to each statement in the alphabetized boxes, there will be one box that is highlighted. If that statement is true for you, that will be the box you highlight.

When you are done going through all of the statements, you need to count how many of each letter you got. This will help you to determine what your answer is for your personality type. You will learn more about what this means in Chapter 6.

Chapter 5: Enneagram Test

#	Statements	A	B	C	D	E	F	G	H	I
1	I have a tendency to be imaginative and romantic.									
	I have a tendency to be down to earth.		√							
2	I have a tendency to take on confrontations head-on.									
	I have a tendency to avoid confrontations.	√								
3	I have a tendency to be charming and ambitious.									
	I have a tendency to be direct and idealistic.				√					
4	I have a tendency to be very intense and focused.								√	
	I have a tendency to be fun-loving and spontaneous.									

5	I have a tendency to be hospitable. I enjoy welcoming new friends into my life.					✓				
	I have a tendency to be very private and sometimes considered to be introverted.									
6	Others find it easy to "get a rise out of me."									
	Others find it hard to "get a rise out of me."	✓								
7	I have a tendency to be considered street smart.									
	I have a tendency to be considered idealistic.			✓						
8	I have a tendency to show affection to the people in my life.									
	I have a tendency to maintain a comfortable distance from people in my life.								✓	
9	If a new experience is presented to me, I									

	will ask myself if it is useful to me.										
	If a new experience is presented to me, I will ask myself if it is enjoyable to me.								✓	
10	I have a tendency to focus far too much on myself and sometimes be considered as self-absorbed or selfish.									
	I have a tendency to focus far too much on others and can sometimes be too generous with my time, energy, and resources.	✓								
11	Others have a tendency to depend on me for my insight and knowledge.								✓	
	Others have a tendency to depend on me for my strength and decisiveness.									
12	I have a tendency of coming across as									

22

	unsure and lacking confidence.	✓							
	I have a tendency to come off as overconfident, maybe even arrogant at times.								
13	I have a tendency to be more relationship-oriented than goal-oriented.				✓				
	I have a tendency to be more goal-oriented than relationship-oriented.								
14	I have a tendency to struggle to speak up for myself.			✓					
	I have a tendency to be outspoken, sometimes even saying things that other people are too scared to say.								
15	I have a tendency to find it hard to commit to one thing and to stop								

#										
	considering alternatives.									
	I have a tendency to find it hard to take it easy and be more flexible in life.			✓						
16	I have a tendency to procrastinate and hesitate before doing anything.	✓								
	I have a tendency to be very bold and domineering over other people.									
17	Sometimes I get in trouble with other people because I am reluctant to get involved with things.									
	Sometimes I get in trouble with other people because I get too involved and have a strong desire to have other people depend on me.						✓			
18	I can usually set my feelings aside so that									

	I can get the job done.		✓							
	I often find myself needing to work through my feelings first in order to get the job done.									
19	I have a tendency to be very methodical and cautious when I am considering what to do.									
	I have a tendency to be risky and adventurous in the actions that I take.									✓
20	I have a tendency to be very supportive and giving, and I enjoy the company of others.					✓				
	I have a tendency to be very serious and reserved. I like discussing problems.									
21	I have a tendency to feel like I have to be the pillar of strength.							✓		

	I have a tendency to feel like I need to be able to perform perfectly.									
22	I like to maintain my independence, and I am okay with asking tough questions.							✓		
	I like to maintain stability and peace of mind.									
23	Sometimes I can be too hard-nosed and skeptical about things.	✓								
	Sometimes I am too soft-hearted and sentimental.									
24	Many times, I find myself worrying that I am missing out on something better.									✓
	Many times, I find myself worrying that if I let down my guard, I will get taken advantage of.									
25	I have a habit of being "stand-offish"									

	to the point that it has annoyed people in my life.									
	I have a habit of telling people what to do to the point that it has annoyed people in my life.			✓						
26	I have a tendency to tune troubles out if they get to me. I do not like intense emotions.	✓								
	I have a tendency to treat myself to an act of self-care if I am experiencing troubles in my life.									
27	I have a tendency to depend on my friends, and they know that they can depend on me, too.		✓							
	I have a tendency to refrain from depending on other people and instead do everything myself.									

28	I have a tendency to be very detached and preoccupied.									
	I have a tendency to be very moody and self-absorbed.			✓						
29	I have a tendency to enjoy challenging people and "shaking them up."									
	I have a tendency to enjoy comforting people and helping them calm down.						✓			
30	I have a tendency to be very outgoing and sociable.									✓
	I have a tendency to be very earnest and self-disciplined.									
31	I have a tendency to be shy, especially when it comes to showing off my abilities.	✓								
	I have a tendency to enjoy letting people see what I am really good at.									

32	It is more important to me to pursue my personal interests than it is for me to pursue comfort and security.								✓	
	It is more important to me to pursue comfort and security than it is to pursue my personal interests.									
33	I have a tendency to withdraw when I am experiencing conflict with other people.				✓					
	I have a tendency to stand strong in my position when I am experiencing conflict with others.									
34	I have a tendency to give up too easily and let other people push me around.	✓								
	I have a tendency to be too uncompromising and even demanding with other people.									

35	People tend to appreciate me more for my sense of humor and unsinkable spirit.									
	People tend to appreciate me more for my quiet strength and generosity.					✓				
36	I believe that much of my success is the result of my talents making a favorable impression on others.			✓						
	I believe that much of my success has been achieved in spite of the fact that I lack interest in developing "interpersonal skills."									

Chapter 6: Enneagram Test Outcome

In order to determine the results of the test, you need to count how many of each letter you have highlighted in the test. You can do so in the table below. Then, based on your results, you can see what your outcome is using the guide beneath the table!

A	B	C	D	E	F	G	H	I
6	5	2	5	4	3	3	4	4

If your highest value is in "A," you are a type nine: The Peacemaker.

If your highest value is in "B," you are a type six: The Loyalist.

If your highest value is in "C," you are a type three: The Achiever.

If your highest value is in "D," you are a type one: The Reformer.

If your highest value is in "E," you are a type four: The Individualist.

If your highest value is in "F," you are a type two: The Helper.

If your highest value is in "G," you are a type eight: The Challenger.

If your highest value is in "H," you are a type five: The Investigator.

If your highest value is in "I," you are a type seven: The Enthusiast.

If you have two with the same value that has tied for your highest value, first ensure that you have answered each question with complete accuracy. Then, consider the type that you personally align most with. This will be your most probable type.

You can learn more about each of these types by browsing parts 4-6 of the remaining portion of this book. In the next section, you will learn about your subtype, which will help you further understand yourself and your personality.

Part 3: Identifying Your Subtype

Chapter 7: What is a Subtype?

Subtypes with the Enneagram types are based on the knowledge that we have three basic instinctual drives that are considered to be essential to the human experience. Each of us carries these three drives. They reside in us on a body-based level, meaning they are primal forces that we are often completely unaware of. The three subtypes, or drives, fall into these categories: self-preservation, one-on-one, and social.

These subtypes are considered to be separate from personality. They are not as pliable as personality is. Instead, they are actually rooted in our life strategies. They are the instinctual drive between what we do and how we do it, as a means to survive.

Each type *will* experience all three subtypes to a varying degree in their lives. However, we have a tendency to experience one subtype more than the other. This would become our primary subtype. It is the one we find easiest to tap into and use, and it tends to influence us far more than the other two. Knowing this information can help you significantly when it comes to understanding your behavior and identity and choosing how to apply your various growth and expression strategies so that you can live your best life.

One way to consider the subtypes that is commonly used in the Enneagram community is this: imagine you are handed a plate with three different types of food. The dominant subtype is the food that you choose to eat first. The secondary subtype is the one you eat next. The least dominant subtype is the one you eat last.

In the following chapters, you are going to learn about all 27 subtypes, based on which type they are related to and what they mean. To determine what your own dominant subtype is, consider which of these you can relate the most and find yourself using most in your life. This will be your probable dominant subtype.

Chapter 8: The Reformer Subtypes

The three subtypes associated with the reformer are worry, zeal, and non-adaptable. You can learn more about these subtypes and what they mean below.

Self-Preservation: Worry

Because of their nature, reformers have a tendency to experience a high amount of worry in their lives. They are often known as perfectionists. They want everything to be under control and completed or managed in a specific way. Therefore, they use worry as a means to anticipate problems or anything that may reduce control or take away things from happening.

It is not uncommon for a reformer to be anxious and excessively prepared for nearly everything in their lives. They have a strong inner critic, with a tendency to be extremely hard on themselves. Many times, they will try to live up to unreasonable standards, and this furthers their worry because they feel they are incapable of achieving these standards.

Although the reformer often avoids expressing angry emotions, they do have a tendency to feel deep levels of frustration when they are disrupted or when things are not up to their standards. This can result in them bottling up a large amount of anger and feeling burdened by their emotions and their perceived failures or the perceived failure of others.

One-on-One: Zeal

Reformers have a very idealistic view on how things should be. They like to try and enroll others in their idealistic view, but rarely want to enroll in the ideas of anyone else. This results in them coming off as intense, and they tend to have a large impact on others. This impact can be positive or negative, depending on who the other person is and how they feel about the idealistic view of the reformer.

When they feel that their efforts are not being improved or resisted by others, the reformer will often become angry and frustrated. This can result in even more bottled up emotions. Alternatively, it can result in conflict and the reformer blaming others for their inability to experience an idealistic reality.

Social: Non-Adaptable

The reformer is known to be non-adaptable. Due to their nature, they believe that their worry combined with their meticulous attention to detail would mean that they are always right. When they are out of balance, they believe that everyone else must be wrong and will often start passing the blame to others when things are not achieved. They have a tendency to reject anyone else's views or beliefs, even those of another reformer.

The reformer typically enjoys drawing attention to what is considered to be good, right, or appropriate. They value integrity and high standards. They are known for a high level of self-control and discipline, and they find themselves both expecting everyone else to live up to their standards, while also wanting to be better than everyone else.

When they are aligned and operating at their best, reformers are rarely bothered by peer pressure and tend to be great role models. They are known to live deep in truth with their beliefs and values. Therefore, they are great at modeling how you can live your best life in alignment with your true self.

Chapter 9: The Helper Subtypes

The three subtypes associated with the helper are: privilege, seduction, and ambition. You can learn more about these subtypes and what they mean below.

Self-Preservation: Privilege

The helper often likes to play coy, seeming as though they need to be taken care of by others. Although they are reluctant to be dependent on another person due to their giving nature, they like to be taken care of. They tend to be very hesitant when taking on commitment, especially on a long-term basis because they worry it will take up a lot of energy based on how much they like to give.

When a helper experiences some level of rejection from another person, they will feel hurt or may even begin to withdraw from that person. This is a form of self-preservation that they feel protects them from being rejected, or abandoned by the people in their lives.

One-on-One: Seduction

Helpers are known to focus on their talents and seductive skills when it comes to build relationships. They use this as an opportunity to create strong relationships, especially intimate ones. When they are in close relationships where they feel trustworthy in the situation, they are more likely to assert their own needs and have them met. When there is balance, there can be a perfect harmony of giving and receiving. When they are in relationships with people they don't know as well, they use their helping and seductive abilities to build the relationship, but will rarely ask for what they need.

Because of their seductiveness, the helper can be strong-willed, flexible, and passionate. Sometimes they are even considered to be wild at heart because of their playfulness. They are known to have very close relationships, and when they do, they are highly devoted to the relationship. They often find it hard to take the word "no" for a definite answer and may find themselves pushing until they get what they want.

Social: Ambition

Through a combination of their seductive tendencies, their privileged ways, and their giving nature, the helper is known to be very ambitious. They are wonderful at engaging with and attracting groups of people, communities, and even global networks. They are known to stand out in a crowd and are typically more than happy to take on the leadership role in a group setting. They love being "in the know," and use their competence and connections to build their influence with other people.

For some helpers, their tendency to give more than they receive may be a way for them to refrain from facing their uncomfortable feelings. If you are dominant in the ambitious subtype, you may not resonate as much with the "childlike" tendency of other helpers. This is because you are more of a leader personality type and like to fully embody that leadership role, which in your mind requires you to refrain from playing in the childlike role of your personality type.

Chapter 10: The Achiever Subtypes

The three subtypes associated with the achiever are: security, charisma, and prestige. You can learn more about these subtypes and what they mean below.

Self-Preservation: Security

The achiever who is dominant in the security subtype will likely refrain from being too "flashy" about their strengths or achievements. They tend to dislike being seen as individuals who are too focused on their image, and instead would like to be recognized for their hard work and the excellence they achieve as a result of that hard work.

The security subtype of the achiever means that they are reliable, productive, and often very efficient at what they do. When they set their mind to something or give you their word, you can feel completely confident that they will do what they have promised to do. They always aspire to do the right thing.

The security-driven achiever desires to be self-sufficient and may find themselves living the lives of a workaholic as they use hard work as a means to get there.

One-on-One: Charisma

Achievers like to use their competitiveness as a way to support other people. They love seeing success in others, as they feel this is a sense of personal success as well, especially if they feel they contributed to the other person's success. If an achiever is dominant in the charismatic subtype, they may base their entire victory based off of the achievement of those around them. Thus, they become heavily invested in other people's triumph.

A charismatic achiever is known to compete for the affection and attention of other people, especially those who are closest to them. They may even find themselves suppressing their own feelings and needs as a way to make themselves appear more attractive to other people. This is so that they can avoid conflict and be seen as more "approachable" and enjoyable. They feel this is a great way for them to improve their likelihood of receiving the most attention and affection from their loved ones.

Social: Prestige

Because of their competitive nature, achievers tend to desire influence. They can be very skillful when it comes to reading situations and adjusting to the social norms of their environment. This makes it so that they can massively impact their influence. This makes them incredible when it comes to being in the spotlight, marketing their ideas, and sharing or promoting their accomplishments.

To the achiever who is dominant in the prestige subtype, they may find themselves needing to look good in front of others. They absolutely crave success, sometimes to the point of cutting corners and covering up failures so that they can appear even more successful. As long as the final outcome makes them and their team look good, the prestigious achiever will be happy.

Chapter 11: The Individualist Subtypes

The three subtypes associated with the individualist are: tenacity, competition, and shame. You can learn more about these subtypes and what they mean below.

Self-Preservation: Tenacity

The tenacious individualist has learned to live with pain so well that they are incredible at making it appear like they are never hurting. Typically, however, this is not true. They tend to suffer internally and keep their negative emotions quiet and to themselves, brooding and bottling it up for as long as possible. They like to be recognized as tough individuals and are great at hiding their complaints or any signs of perceived weakness to maintain this exterior image.

The dominant tenacious individualist is still just as emotional as the other two subtypes, often being discreetly sensitive. They tend to disconnect from their feelings as a means to hide them, as a way to keep their image clean and tough. They do not like to share their pain with other people. Because of their deep suffering, the tenacious individualist tends to be empathic and can sense the suffering in other people. As a result, they are always looking out for others and do their best to support anyone else who is suffering.

One-on-One: Competition

An individualist can be extremely intense and very vocal about their feelings and needs. They can be shameless in getting what they want or need, sometimes even by being demanding. Individualists are also known for being competitive, using their achievements and abilities as a way to escape the suffering that they feel inside. By distracting themselves with their abilities and being the best at what they do, they feel that they can suppress the emotions that they are feeling.

Stemming from their competitiveness, the individualist that is dominant in the competitive subtype often demands that other people appreciate their needs. This typically results in them feeling rejected, angry, and frustrated. They may even use their anger as a way to mask how sad they are truly feeling. To them, the angry expression shows more strength and toughness than a sad one.

Social: Shame

Just like the other two subtypes, individualists who have the dominant subtype of shame are very emotional. These ones, in particular, are deeply connected to the suffering that they are experiencing. They actually find comfort in suffering and will often express this to others. Sometimes, they even use their suffering and shame as a way to command support and admiration from other people.

Unlike the other two subtypes, those dominant in shame tend to lack the competitive tendency. However, they do have a deeply rooted desire to be completely understood for the true nature of who they really are inside. They are known to doubt themselves, see themselves as inferior to others, and compare themselves to others then blame themselves for not being "good enough." This results in this subtype living with strong feelings of shame and envy for others.

Chapter 12: The Investigator Subtypes

The three subtypes associated with the investigator are castle, confidant, and totem. You can learn more about these subtypes and what they mean below.

Self-preservation: Castle

The investigator has a tendency to be very protective over their privacy and their personal space. They are known for having very clear boundaries and limits and tend to enjoy living their life in a solitary manner. The investigator may only have very few close friends, and no one else can be noteworthy in their life. This allows them to keep themselves preserved and ensures that the individuals they are interacting with will definitely adhere to their strict personal boundaries.

Investigators often find themselves preferring to observe others socializing or living their lives versus actually doing it themselves. They are typically the truest form of introvert to exist. They do not typically prefer to reveal themselves to other people, as they find it difficult to do so. They like to keep their guard up to refrain from losing their privacy or the security they experience by staying solitary and with strict boundaries.

One-on-One: Confidant

Due to the solitary and quiet nature of the investigator, they tend to be very passionate about and loyal to the few close people that they have in their lives. They will typically find themselves experiencing a strong chemistry with those close in their lives and find enjoyment in the level of intensity that this brings to their relationship. This allows them to feel very trustworthy and open to their close ones.

The investigator will risk the feeling of depending on the other people they are close with as a way to make them feel vibrant and alive in their lives. This can result in them periodically "testing" the loyalty of those in their lives to see if the same intensity is returned. They may even become possessive and resist sharing these people with anyone else.

Social: Totem

Investigators are known to look for the deeper or hidden meaning in virtually every situation. They ask big questions and love to pursue wisdom and seek greater levels of knowledge. They are typically highly passionate about connecting with groups or specific experts who are brilliant in the topics that the investigator is most passionate about. Although they love sharing in these group settings, they may resist sharing any of their space, time, or resources too much. Instead, they prefer to absorb, observe, and learn from others while quietly accumulating their own knowledge.

They tend to be quite disconnected from everyday emotions and issues that the average person faces. They may even find themselves disconnecting from people around them altogether, preferring to preserve their energy to learn more.

Chapter 13: The Loyalist Subtypes

The three subtypes associated with the loyalist are warmth, intimidation, and duty. You can learn more about these subtypes and what they mean below.

Self-Preservation: Warmth

Loyalists have a tendency to be very anxious, which results in them feeling fearful and insecure. They become extremely cautious of most situations, including circumstantial and social. As a result of this tendency, the loyalist will often create a sense of security by building strong, reliable alliances and relationships with other people in their lives.

The loyalist is a truly warm-hearted and affectionate person, so the relationships they form on the basis of their warm nature is sincere and true. Sometimes, however, they will repress their anger and may be hesitant to share their true opinions, feelings, or beliefs with others to refrain from causing conflict. They prefer to be cautious and kind towards everyone so that they don't lose the people in their lives, rather than being honest and risking the conflict.

One-on-One: Intimidation

Another way of keeping themselves in a state of feeling secure instead of anxious and fearful is by being bold and intimidating toward others. The loyalist may be known to be excessively assertive over their opinions, beliefs, and feelings as a way to defend themselves and stay on the offense. They are typically quite reactive.

Rather than running away from fear, the loyalist with the intimidating subtype will run directly at it as an attempt to confront it and win every single time. They can be rebellious and even a daredevil with this subtype as a result of their need to feel strong and safe.

When a loyalist is living dominantly in the intimidation subtype, they may struggle to make connections with other people or have close friends as a result. This can result in them having greater doubts, feelings of vulnerability, and fears around relationships. This can be painful for the secretly sensitive intimidating loyalist.

Social: Duty

If a loyalist is dominant in the subtype of duty, they are known to be passionate about standing up for the underdog. When they see someone as weak or incapable of fully standing up for themselves, they will take it upon themselves to stand up for them. They may become highly passionate in charitable work or other activist-based activities.

Loyalists with the duty subtype typically like to follow rules and predetermined procedures and are often precise and very careful in their actions to ensure that they are doing things right. They feel a strong sense of duty for others and are typically operating from a highly rational state. These loyalists have a strong sense for justice and like to encourage others to bide by the rules as well. They are also great at making sure that everyone else knows what is expected of them.

Chapter 14: The Enthusiast Subtypes

The three subtypes associated with the enthusiast are network, fascination, and sacrifice. You can learn more about these subtypes and what they mean below.

Self-Preservation: Network

The enthusiast loves to network. They are incredibly effective at it and typically gather what they consider to be a "family" of close supporters. They are motivated by their desire for everyone to have and experience the best. Networking enthusiasts love to enjoy good things in life and will often risk building a reputation as self-interested and pleasure-seeking in order to do so.

The networking enthusiast tends to be great at getting what they want and need, especially when it comes to having fun and feeling safe. They also have a tendency to be really good at rationalizing what they want to do, defending their right to have fun, and thus taking risks that others may see as irrational.

One-on-One: Fascination

The enthusiast who is dominant in the subtype of fascination is known to be a true "life through rose-colored glasses" type. They are dreamers, romantics, and idealists. They love to connect to the possibility in everything, often rejecting the reality of it to do so. These enthusiasts are often seen as unrealistic or naïve as a result of their optimism. They believe in the good in everything and everyone, which is not how many other types see the world.

Enthusiasts who are dominant in the subtype of fascination typically prefer to see the world in an embellished way to avoid seeing it as dreary and dull. They want everything to be enjoyable, including their reality. This can result in them disliking being stuck in relationships that are boring or predictable.

Social: Sacrifice

This is considered to be a countertype to the typical enthusiast. Rather than being gluttonous, they have a strong desire to be of service and are considered to be generous givers. They want to create a better world and will give much of themselves in favor of this dream of theirs.

If they are dominant in the sacrificing subtype, enthusiasts will sacrifice their own needs and desires as a way to serve their intended audience. These enthusiasts are known to become judgmental towards those who are perceived by them as selfish and want to be appreciated and known for their sacrifice.

Chapter 15: The Challenger Subtypes

The three subtypes associated with the challenger are satisfaction, possession, and solidarity. You can learn more about these subtypes and what they mean below.

Self-Preservation: Satisfaction

Challengers have a tendency to be extremely confident. Their personality type is strong, productive, and direct. They are known as powerful and effective individuals. They have a strong survivor instinct and regularly take on the role of a guardian for many others, often being seen as a motherly or fatherly figure to those in their lives.

The downside to this strong tendency in the challenger type is that they can quickly become frustrated or intolerant if their needs are not being met. Because they are typically so good at meeting their own needs, this can create a feeling of distress or internal chaos in the challenger. When they do reach this state of intolerance, they can become very direct in their approach of having their needs met. They're known to be unapologetic and to show no remorse for the tactics they use to get their needs met.

One-on-One: Possession

When a challenger is dominant in the subtype of possession, they have a tendency to break rules and become rebellious. They may even become a trail blazer. These individuals can be impulsive and intense, with a strong desire to create change. The actions they take in creating this change are often rooted in an unapologetic nature. Challengers are nearly always willing to disrupt others and the system in order to gain power and influence, which they then use to make change. A challenger who is in this position strongly desires serving for a worthy cause, though they rarely want to do so from a "standby" position. They would rather be in charge or playing a highly central role in making it happen.

If a challenger is out of balance with their subtype of possession, they are likely to become excessively challenging toward the "system." This can result in chaos or destruction, as not every system was made to be disrupted. They may become restless and frustrated, and their powerful and confident nature may become obsessive and slightly aggressive as they push too hard to be in control.

Social: Solidarity

When the challenger is in balance and in a place of service, they may be dominant in the subtype of solidarity. They can be fiercely loyal to people or causes, often going out of their way to have the needs of the other person or cause met. They exercise the same confidence and power that they use to have their own needs met and use this as a means to get the needs of the others met, too.

The challenger tends to be highly sensitive towards injustice and will fight for fairness for all. They dislike unfair social norms and will use their disruptive tendency to shake things up and create chaos if need be, as a means to help them balance things back into a just fashion. Although the challenger prefers to refrain from being in a vulnerable position, they will invite tough feedback from close allies. In fact, they appreciate these types of feedback because it encourages them to do better.

Chapter 16: The Peacemaker Subtypes

The three subtypes associated with the peacemaker are appetite, fusion, and participation. You can learn more about these subtypes and what they mean below.

Self-Preservation: Appetite

The peacemaker is known for having their physical needs met. They're very into consumption. They consume foods, hobbies, and comforting activities regularly as a way to keep themselves feeling harmoniously balanced. They may also use these as an escape or comforting strategy to help them face difficulties they are facing in their lives. They have an appetite for peace and harmony and are willing to do almost anything to satisfy that appetite.

The peacemaker is known to love peace and alone time, and they can become irritable and frustrated when they don't have enough. They may even become stubborn and resist doing anything with the other people as a means to attempt to balance their own needs. They may intentionally create problems with others so that they have an excuse to storm off and retreat to a more peaceful, isolated environment.

One-on-One: Fusion

The peacemaker tends to fuse themselves deeply when in relationships. They fuse to the other person, using this as a strategy to create comfort and feed their sense of self. When they are partnered with another individual, they feel more secure. When they are completely alone, they tend to feel vulnerable and uncomfortable. The peacemaker *does* crave and value peaceful alone time, but they do like to have a significant other in their lives. This is likely because they prefer to be very close with one person, rather than slightly close to many.

The peacemaker has a tendency to resist paying attention to themselves, often choosing to pay attention to someone else and the other person's needs and desires instead. They tend to absorb all of their together-time and alone-time in being concerned with everyone else's needs and not their own. They would rather go along with the preferences and desires of their loved ones than go along with their own, even if this means sacrificing their own needs and requirements.

Social: Participation

When the peacemaker is dominant in the subtype of participation, they tend to be highly friendly and sociable. They like to lean in and be fully invested in whatever they are doing with other people. They are known to take the role of the mediator or facilitator in groups, as their peacemaking nature helps them ensure that everyone gets along and works together smoothly.

Being completely invested in social situations means that the peacemaker can put their own issues aside and focus on making everyone else happy. This helps them further walk away from their own problems and invest themselves in something else that gives them a sense of meaning and significance. They take comfort in these groups and often work hard to keep everyone else happy. They may even become a workaholic or a master in hiding their own distress as a means to serve everyone else.

Part 4: Introduction to the Centers

Chapter 17: What is a "Center"?

The Enneagram is broken up by what is called triads or fractals. These break the nine types into three centers. Although these centers are standard, they may be expressed in three different ways for each individual.

The centers are used to describe three points of contact through which we become present in our reality. In order for us to be deeply rooted in our reality, we need to connect more with these three centers. The more we become present with the center, the more we can integrate ourselves and our self-expression at a higher level of development. From this higher level, the center can be transformed into a powerful tool to be used by the individual.

When it comes to your journey with the Enneagram, you have to be mindful of these centers. This will ensure that you are aware of what is required for you to be more attuned with what you need in order to develop. It is through these three points that you will develop who you are, deepen your relationships, and express yourself with greater certainty, authenticity, and confidence.

The three centers you are going to learn that exist on the Enneagram include the action center, the feeling center, and the thinking center. Let's explore these centers in greater depth, now.

Chapter 18: The Action Center

The action center is, as you expect, where action is taken. You experience or engage in action through your hands, instinct, body, and gut. This means that any time you engage in action; you are activating the action center.

The action center *loves* movement. It will encourage you to move, experience, and engage with the environment around you. It often works on a subconscious level, when you are instinctually drawn to do something. Often, the action center is looking out for your physical survival.

When you are subconsciously or unconsciously working with the action center, you will find yourself taking action that may be destructive or seemingly uncalculated. This is because you are acting on an impulse and often without thinking. These actions will likely be aligned with your unique personality type, which means that the impulsive actions taken by each individual may vary.

For example, a challenger who has not mastered their action center may impulsively act toward defeating "the system" without taking calculated action. They may become disruptive and destructive in an unhealthy way, leading to negative consequences for the challenger. Alternatively, a peacemaker may compulsively take action toward making others happy through becoming a people pleaser, thus ignoring their own needs and facing consequences in that way.

When it is balanced, and you are consciously taking advantage of the action center's intelligence, the action center serves as a great tool. This is where calculated, intentional action stems from. It allows you to be very clear in your action, thus giving you the opportunity to grow, develop, and evolve along your life path. The actions you take are typically productive and efficient, warranting great results from your action.

A person who is dominant in the action center through their expression is typically known to have what is called "hot" energy. This means they take a lot of action, operate off their instincts, and are charged by physical sensations. Physical sensations can have a major impact on whether they will choose to act or not, and how they will act if they choose to take action. A person who experiences a strong action center tends to be very energetic and lively. They can come off as intense or even aggressive, as the action-dominant individual is generally driven by some degree of anger. If they are operating at an unproductive level, they may be intense in their actions and very unclear in their desired outcomes. They act impulsively. If they are expressed in an intelligent manner, they are likely to show up with the gift of power, energy, and decisiveness. They will have clear intention on their desired outcome and will also have great power in achieving that desired outcome.

Someone who is dominant in the action center and is expressing it intelligently will have a grounded vibe. Even though they are highly energetic and somewhat intense, they will still seem very rational and down-to-earth, because they are. They tend to be very aligned with doing activities that keep their body strong and healthy, so they are known for being outgoing.

The most common personality types to be dominant in the action center include the reformer, the challenger, and the peacemaker. These individuals tend to be driven by their desire to take action and make changes. These individuals will be motivated by different factors, but their methods of execution will be similar in that they take action to achieve their desired results. They are more physically involved and invested in their lives than other types on the Enneagram.

Chapter 19: The Feeling Center

The feeling center is dominated by the heart, emotions, relationships, and purpose. This includes giving and receiving feelings, as well as monitoring and experiencing the overall feelings that someone experiences in their lives.

For many people, the feeling center can be described as warm and comfortable. When considering feelings, the average person will want to ensure that they feel good and content. However, their *need* to feel good will vary based on their personality type. For example, an enthusiast does everything with the intention of feeling good, whereas an achiever is willing to risk their comfort in favor of achieving their desired goals.

Feelings are generated from various experiences in an individual's life. They can come from relationships, past experiences, memories, activity that the individual is engaging in, or any other number of things. It is important to understand that feelings directly contribute to an individual's instinct as well. Therefore, individuals will regularly act based on their feelings.

When a person is dominant in their feeling center, it is regularly expressed through a warm energy and emotional self-awareness. These individuals are more emotionally available for connection and relationships with other individuals. When individuals express themselves dominantly through feelings, they are typically seen as open-hearted and sensitive. They are excellent at connecting to the needs of others, sometimes even more so than the other individuals.

When an individual is highly expressed through their feeling center, they have a tendency to be very inclusive when they are solving problems. Rather than doing it independently, they will regularly choose to involve others who are or are not involved in the situation. They like to ensure that all involved are being treated fairly and in a way that is emotionally gentle. Often, someone who is dominant in the feeling center will collaborate with others, which can expand their perception so that they feel confident that they are acting in everyone's best interest when solving the said problem.

If a person who is dominant in the feeling center is out of balance or not acting from a place of conscious awareness and intention, they often become over-sensitive or even volatile. They may use emotional manipulation as a means to get other people on their side and to have their emotional needs met. This can result in them feeling particularly drained, as they are feeling the negative repercussion of their own emotional harshness. This means that they are suffering while also causing others to suffer, which can result in even deeper rooted suffering for this individual.

When the feeling center is balanced, the individual is often known for their empathic abilities. They are known for being highly receptive of other's needs and are authentic in their ability to express their emotions. They can express emotions and give and receive emotional feedback without feeling knocked off or otherwise misaligned with their center. They are known to be emotionally intelligent and mature, and are great at understanding, identifying, and processing their own emotions. They are also incredible at helping others do the same, as they genuinely understand when they listen to the emotional experiences of other individuals. They offer true support and genuine guidance, often in a way that is aligned with the best interest of the individual they are talking to. People will often describe these individuals as possessing "heart intelligence."

The most common personality types to be dominant in their feeling centers include the helper, the achiever, and the individualist. Because of their natures, each of these personality types are best known for being centered on their feelings. Each type, however, will experience and express their feelings in a highly personalized manner. This means that not everyone will be the same in how they experience, balance, or express their emotions. However, they will each likely be driven by their emotions more than their actions or thoughts.

Chapter 20: The Thinking Center

The thinking center represents the head, logic, brain, and information. This is where people create and store thoughts, memories, and experiences in their mind. When you are learning, you are activating and using the thinking center. The thinking center is known to have a cool energy and is related to rationality and logic.

The thinking center is the one responsible for helping people plan, prepare, and prioritize. These individuals are great logical thinkers, tend to act very rationally when they are balanced and are known for their ability to solve complex problems with a variety of unique solutions.

Thoughts are a major part of life and being able to confidently and effectively use your thinking as a tool in your life is a powerful measure. This is responsible for our evolution as humans, as without the thought center we would be highly driven by instinct and less likely to develop as much knowledge throughout our lifetime. The human brain, as you already know, is a highly evolved tool that has assisted humans in advancing through many stages in life.

Clearly, it is an important tool. Just as important as action and feelings!

Individuals who are dominant in the thinking center are more likely to act based on thoughts than they are on the other two centers. This means that while they are still highly driven by instinct, they are typically able to discern instinct from thoughts when they are balanced. They are excellent at planning things, formulating many different ideas, exercising their imagination, storing and processing information, using rational thinking, and prioritizing virtually everything in their lives from their thoughts to their feelings and actions.

When people are dominant in their thinking center, they are excellent at analyzing. This can be a powerful tool, though if left unbalanced or used unconsciously, can lead to analysis paralysis. This means that the person has analyzed so much that they essentially scare themselves from taking any action. They get stuck in a chronic state of taking in and processing more information, feeling that it is never quite the "right time" to act on this information. They love to have a solid understanding of facts and a clear understanding of what is going on around them. The more they know, the better they feel.

If the thinking center is unbalanced, the individual may begin to over-plan things. This can lead to them delaying decisions and using their thoughts and rationale as a means to try and control situations. This can be particularly frustrating to the individual when the situation is truly beyond their control. They may also be prone to excessive worry, anxiety, doubt, harsh self-criticism, and fear as they are stuck in the analysis paralysis state.

If the thinking center is balanced, the individual is known to be curious, calm, and clear when it comes to taking action in life. They are excellent at reflecting on things but are also excellent at moving through thoughts and decisions and into action. They can be highly efficient and effective, often making great leaders and mentors in life. The individual that is controlled by the thought center is known to be a very intelligent one. In the Enneagram, these individuals are described as having "head intelligence."

The individuals that are most likely to have a dominant thinking center are those who have the personality types of the investigator, the loyalist, or the enthusiast. These individuals tend to be very "in their head" most of their lives, living predominantly through thoughts, observation, analysis, and imagination rather than anything else.

Part 5: Self-Awareness and Growth Potential for Each Type

Chapter 21: The Reformer

The reformer is known to value principles and integrity the most. Their motivation typically lies in being good and being right. Individuals who are reformers are known to strive for perfection and seek self-control as a means to reach it. They are highly disciplined and always strive to be better than themselves and, often times, everyone else as well.

Things to Become Aware Of

When the reformer is balanced, they tend to be tolerant, serene, and self-accepting. They seek to give their best to everything without compromising their self-worth. In other words, they can accept where they are, while still seeking to achieve better and not being critically harsh on themselves.

When the reformer is out of balance, they become harsh critics of themselves and the world around them. Their own need for perfection can become a major source of anxiety and stress in their lives, and they have a hypersensitivity toward self-awareness and their own perceived flaws. They can be highly judgmental, unwilling to compromise, and continually feel as though they themselves and those around them are not good enough.

If you are a reformer, your gifts are magnificent. You are known to be principled, objective, conscientious, structured, and quality-minded. You value integrity and always want to lead individuals through example, by showing up as your best self while continually striving to do better. As a result, you'll make a great leader. You are able to see and judge situations without emotions, meaning you can get an honest account of all sides of the story and work from a place of rational thinking, instead of an emotion-driven place that could result in one-sidedness or selfishness. You are known to be reliable and responsible, as you always see things through until the very end. If you give your word, people can guarantee that you are going to follow through. You love structure. When things are structured, you feel as though everyone has a common goal to work towards it, and has a specific way to get there. This means everyone stays on track. This heavily contributes to your ability to ensure that everything is achieved with high-quality standards, which are your expectation every time, with everything that you do.

Typically, reformers have a very internalized action pattern. Their actions are rooted in self-discipline, self-control, and acting in alignment with principle. Their principles are highly valued by them, and as a result others often regard the reformer as responsible, critical, and organized. Due to their internalized action patterns, reformers are great at planning and organizing, even with seemingly challenging tasks. They are excellent at producing structure in all that they do, as this helps them ensure everyone is working with the same high-quality standards that they are.

The typical thinking patterns for reformers are deeply rooted in "right" and "wrong." As a result of their principled nature, they have a tendency to view things one way or the other and always fight for everything to be right. They also tend to live in the belief that if they or someone else cannot commit to doing something correctly, they should not do it at all. Everything should be done properly in alignment with their high standards. Otherwise, it is just a waste of time.

Reformers are known to be deeply engaged in internal conversations that are rooted in improvement. Their self-talk often includes stuff like "I have to," "I should," and "I must." They create a personal set of rules, and their entire thinking and inner dialogue patterns revolve around ensuring that these rules are adhered to at all times. This is how they are able to ensure strong self-discipline, but can also be where the stress and anxiety start if the reformer is not living in a place of balance. When the rules they have created are designed to expand and grow, they can be powerful and helpful. When they are excessive or constricting their lives, this is when anxiety and discomfort surfaces for the reformer.

As a result of being so deeply devoted to their personal rules and values, reformers often seek out friends and groups of people who are able to allow them to express their needs. They like spending time with groups whose rules align with theirs, as this ensures that they do not need to justify or convince others to believe in their rules.

The feelings of a reformer are quite vast, though they tend to experience a large amount of anger and frustration in their life. Even so, they rarely express this anger toward anyone, as this would likely contradict the rules they have made for themselves. This anger typically exists because their rules are their own and not everyone else in their life will adhere to them. This leads to major internal battles of right versus wrong which, for the reformer, is a very challenging battle to face.

Even though the reformer works hard to refrain from expressing their anger and tend to appear reserved and collected most of the time if they experience a moment of intense frustration they will typically express it. This generally happens when they are surrounded by people who do not have the same high standards as them, or who have excessively lower standards of quality. If the reformer perceives someone to be irresponsible, they will also develop resentment and frustration towards that person.

When a reformer does choose to express his anger, it is typically done in a strategic way. He tends to be excellent at finding many ways to justify the anger he expressed, even if it was expressed in a poor manner in a moment of heat.

The blind spots that reformers often experience can be a challenge for them to admit to since these typically fall outside of the lines of their rules. Since there is no way for them to perfectly put them in the boxes of "right" or "wrong," they may choose to ignore it altogether. One blind spot that reformers often have is their inability to realize that they have a tendency to be highly impatient and critical of others. They want things done right and fast. They attempt to be constructive toward the other person but may come across as rude and pushy instead. They are generally not clear on how much their anger and resentment come through in body language. Though they may be verbally expressing themselves in a more collected manner, physically they may be showing obvious signs of their displeasure. When they do feel righteous about an issue, a reformer will regularly struggle to see from any other point of view. They believe they are right and no other opinions or otherwise exist. Therefore, anyone who tries to have their opposing opinions or beliefs shared will likely be completely ignored by the reformer. If the reformer feels particularly sensitive or passionate about the topic, that individual may even experience the nastiness of the reformer's anger.

A great way to ensure that you are self-aware of yourself as a reformer is to pay attention to these tendencies and begin to recognize how they show up for you in your life. When you take the time to explore these tendencies and recognize them, especially those that lie in your blind spot, it can become a lot easier for you to understand where improvements can be made.

It is also important to understand and begin to recognize when you are feeling unbalanced in your expression. You will likely notice this through a particularly harsh inner critic, excessive judgment toward others, or excessive anxiety. When these arise, you will probably notice that your reformer tendencies are out of balance and that you need to bring awareness to this topic.

Growth Potential

The biggest area of growth potential that many reformers need to pay attention to is their inner critic. Due to their need to be right all of the time, the critic can become unruly and unkind if the reformer is not careful and paying attention to it. By paying attention and healing the harshness of this inner critic, it can be a lot easier for reformers to cut themselves some slack in their lives. This does not mean that you need to skimp out on your attention to quality and detail. Instead, it means that you do not bully yourself if you make a mistake or something isn't done up to your usual high standards.

It is also important that you focus on dealing with your anger and inner frustration. Keeping these emotions bottled up will only result in further stress and anxiety, and is often the cause of reformers becoming anxious and fixated on their personal rules. Giving yourself a generous amount of time to process and heal these emotions as you experience them through an effective outlet can ensure that you are not bottling these emotions up and suffering as a result. It will also help you come across more soft and warm to your audience, as you will not be fighting to hold them down since they are not within you, weighing you down.

Lastly, it is important that you set the intention of giving your audience a voice. As a reformer, it can be a challenge for you to sit back and let other people share their opinions without you arguing against their opinion. This is because, often, other people's opinions do not fit your ideal of right versus wrong. It is important to understand that your set of personal rules that you live by and what you use to judge things as "right" will not always be the same as other people's. You will gain a lot more traction if you listen to other people and honor their right to their own opinion, then share yours as opposed to arguing to try and get them on your side or outright dismissing them because they are not on the same page as you.

Chapter 22: The Helper

The helper is motivated by their need to be appreciated by others and liked by others. Their values lie in their relationships with others and ensuring that they come across as generous, kind, and self-sacrificing. The highest goal of a helper tends to be within their desire to make the world a better, loving place. They do this by offering their attention and generous support to the people whom they care about the most.

Things to Become Aware Of

When the helper is balanced, they are known to be unconditionally supportive of their loved ones. They are able to do this while also ensuring that their own needs are met through powerful self-care. They are able to easily give themselves the same generous, loving support and attention that they give to their loved ones. As a result, they give even more because they are pouring from a full cup.

When the helper is out of balance, they can become very toxic in relationships. They may give only with the intention of receiving and may give too much because they are pouring out of an empty vessel. Their ability to practice self-care dwindles, and they may struggle to spend any time alone with themselves due to unhappy and uncomfortable emotions. The helper that is unbalanced tends to have low self-worth and believes that they are not worthy of love. They may feel like they have to be a certain type of person or behave a specific way in order to receive love.

Helpers are very gifted when it comes to community. They are known to be warm in their personality, generous and giving, people-centered, sacrificing, and praising. They love to ensure that everyone feels supported and cherished. Typically, the helper will be one of your biggest cheerleaders when you accomplish something in your life. They love to stand in your corner and celebrate your wins with you. The helper can also be highly empathic and excellent at anticipating the needs of others. They know how to take care of these needs for others in many cases too, often before the person even knows. Great networkers, the helper loves to build relationships. Not just any relationships, though. Helpers love to be invested in deep relationships that are mutually beneficial.

The typical feeling pattern of a helper is that they love to feel helpful and needed. They are at their best when they are able to assist others, and therefore, they make themselves highly available to those around them. By others, the helper is regularly perceived as someone who is warm-hearted, considerate, friendly, and generous. They are known to live from their hearts which allows them to project unconditional love and support to those around them.

A helper is known to have a great sense of empathy. This means they are particularly gifted at knowing what another person needs through feeling them, and that they are able to anticipate how they can help others. This makes them a great supportive friend to have.

Something that generally surprises people about the feeling pattern of a helper is that they actually tend to carry a fiery temper. They do not often show this temper, as they are not one to feel angry often. However, when they feel that they are being taken advantage of or that someone is undervaluing them as a person, they can become extremely frustrated in a short matter of time. This can result in a great deal of resentfulness and pain for the helper, resulting in them acting from a place of temperamental anger.

Even though the helper is known for loving helping other people, they still like to be valued and have the loving support returned to them. The balanced helper is particularly skilled at creating and building friendships and relationships with people who value them and who are willing to engage in a mutually supportive, loving, and beneficial relationship. The challenge that a helper will sometimes face, however, is that they do not want to ask for their loving, generous support to be returned. Instead, they prefer that the other party in the relationship simply recognize their need for attention and appreciation and they express it accordingly. If they feel that they have been brushed off by the other party, the helper may then end up experiencing their fiery anger and a deep sense of emotional pain.

The action patterns that are typically experienced and expressed by the helper tend to make them excellent at networking. They are great when it comes to having deep friendships and many of them. Helpers love to shower their close friends, and virtually everyone else, with compliments and support. They regularly praise the people in their lives, offering words of encouragement and celebration everywhere that they possibly can.

Each helper has their own unique method for expressing their appreciation for the people in their life. This way is their personal way of ensuring that everyone feels valued, loved, and cherished. Helpers tend to act most when they feel action is needed. They anticipate what is needed and then act on that.

One of the best ways a helper expresses their actions is through giving advice, fulfilling favors for people, and giving a helping hand whenever possible. They love to express and provide support through action, whether it is verbal or physical. If someone needs a shoulder to cry on, a helper is a great person to turn to. Likewise, if you have an errand you need help running or completing, the helper will help in any way they feel they possibly can. They are typically quick to hop into action the moment they know they are needed.

When it comes to their thinking patterns, the helper is very considerate of others. As you now know, they are finely attuned to the needs of others through their empathic gifts. They can often predict or anticipate the need of another before the other individual even does. This contributes to their need to help others, and their values of being generous, kind, and self-sacrificing in relationships.

As a result of their tendency to prefer, crave, and need connection, the helper's mind is typically consumed with thoughts of others. They use their thoughts to search for ways to become more valuable to other people. This means that they do not spend a lot of time considering their own needs or desires, which can quickly result in the helper feeling drained. The helper does have a great sense of pride and self-worth, but this is gained and expanded through ensuring that they are available to help others and that they put other people first. Their sense of personal value is rooted in how they can be of service to others.

Helpers, as you can probably suspect, have blind spots rooted in various areas that involve other people and relationships. For example, they don't always recognize where the true intention of their generosity comes from. They tend to be highly caring and supportive, but don't realize that this comes from a need to be valued and depended on by others. This, when left unrecognized, can result in the helper feeling like they are pursuing empty relationships and drained.

Another blind spot helpers have is that they can quickly disengage with another individual as soon as they lose interest. This typically happens when they no longer feel like they can help the other person. When they believe their "job is done," and the other person is no longer important to them, the helper will move on to the next person instead. This is driven by a fear of not being needed by someone else and a need to be a strong support in other's lives.

Something many helpers face frequently is that they end up filling their plate to the brim. . As an attempt to help others and to fulfill their deeply rooted need to be helpful, they may take on far too many tasks and become overwhelmed and confused. This can result in the helper experiencing serious burnout, which can be painful for them to face.

Lastly, a major blind spot that helpers face is when it comes to being aware of their own needs and desires. Because they devote so much of their lives, feelings, thoughts, and actions to other people, they may find themselves feeling neglected and uncared for. This is because they are not caring for their own needs and, due to their nature of being needed, may also be in relationships where they feel the intensity of support and emotion is not being returned to them.

The best way for the helper to become more self-aware is to begin recognizing areas in their life where they are experiencing that need to help others. They should also spend time becoming aware of how they can ensure that they are supporting themselves as well as others, so they do not end up giving too much of their time and energy to others and burning out.

Growth Potential

Your biggest growth potential as a helper lies in ensuring that you are living in the balanced helper type. This means that you need to ensure that you are paying attention to your own feelings, needs, and desires as well as that of others. Your nature is rooted in helping others, but it is essential that you remain mindful to the fact that you cannot help others if you are living in a state of personal neglect. Be cautious of times when you choose to hide your own needs in favor of fulfilling someone else's. This can quickly lead to hurt and resentment, as you try too hard to fulfill your needs vicariously through someone else.

You also need to make sure that you don't take on too much. As a helper, you may find yourself feeling overwhelmed or burnt out because you take on the responsibility of helping too many people and fulfilling too many favors at once. Be realistic about your time and energy, and be cautious about over-promising your resources. Keeping your plate this full is often the result of you trying to avoid your own needs or feelings, so anytime you find yourself in this pattern, ask yourself where *your* needs require priority and being met. It is likely that you are avoiding them on some level, and that is resulting in you overburdening yourself with too much to do.

It is also important that you assess the motivations behind your relationships. Ensure that you are not in them as an attempt to "fix" the other person. Give yourself the opportunity to learn how you can stay engaged in relationships even after they lose their "interesting" factor. Although you do not need to spend all of your time with people who do not make your life feel full, you also want to make sure that you are not disengaging from relationships and starving yourself of the value of deep, personal connections that are mutually enjoyable.

Lastly, understand that not everyone shows their love and support in the same way you do. By giving yourself the love and support that you need and cherishing others as they are, it becomes easier for you to avoid getting hurt. This is the better choice over completely ignoring emotions altogether, or overwhelming yourself to avoid them. When you honor your own needs and put yourself first, you ensure that you are not leaving yourself open to being hurt by other's inability to fulfill a need within you.

Chapter 23: The Achiever

Achievers are motivated by their desire and need to be the best at everything they do. They hold efficiency, results, and recognition as highly important in their lives. They want to be successful in all that they do, and have a tendency to choose to work in fields that challenge them and that, when they succeed, can be worn as a badge of status. The achiever is willing to do virtually anything to achieve their goals.

Things to Become Aware Of

When an achiever is balanced, they are principled, receptive, hard-working individuals. They are passionate about offering hope and integrity to the world through all that they do. This allows them to fulfill their need to be the best, but it comes across in a way that serves everyone. They will be competitive, but not in a harsh or bitter way. Instead, they will likely be competitive against themselves and with the desire to do their best and be their best at all times.

When an achiever is out of balance, they can become harsh and arrogant in how they carry themselves. They begin to become overly critical of themselves and others and can pass harsh judgment around at an incredibly high rate. They hold a high standard for themselves, sometimes intentionally putting it at an unachievable height to fulfill a self-fulfilling prophecy that they are not good enough. They also become very self-absorbed in continuing to try to reach those unreasonable standards, while still being unkind and feeling unfulfilled.

Achievers are highly gifted individuals. They are known to be the "athlete" of the personality types because they are full of ambition, driven, efficient, adaptable, and results-oriented. They set goals, and they will go to nearly any length to ensure that their goals are met. They are known to be highly resourceful and are willing to adapt along the way to ensure that their goals are met. They love to get things done and are focused on having high-quality results woven into everything that they do in their lives.

When it comes to their action patterns, achievers are known as "doers." They can stay focused on the task that they are actively trying to accomplish and are excellent at prioritizing and taking action as needed. They bring a great amount of energy to the table when it comes to their action, which further supports them in achieving their goals. One major way achievers act is by adapting to the situation at hand. They are excellent at adapting to any set of circumstances or individuals that are around them, sometimes even being known as "chameleons." They are gifted at using this adaptability to impress virtually anyone they need to in order to achieve their goals. The achiever likes to incorporate their desire and need for success in every area of their life, which can be seen even in the way that they dress. They truly love being prepared for the success that they feel is inevitable in their lives.

In their personal and recreational lives, many achievers are drawn to activities that provide them with the opportunity to continue to challenge themselves. For example, they are likely to be interested in competitive sports or team-based activities that allow them to set a goal, challenge themselves, and win. They tend to be captains and team leaders given their nature and they thrive in these leadership roles.

An achiever's thinking patterns are often rooted in framing and reframing circumstances to either help them learn a lesson or quickly correct a problem. They are excellent at solving even the most complex problem in minimal timing through their ability to think, see the entire problem, frame and reframe it as needed, and search for the opportunities to learn and grow.

As logical thinkers, achievers tend to be very data-oriented. They love to know, use, and learn about facts and knowledge. Learning is one of their favorite things to do. When they find information that directly supports what they need or what they are trying to achieve, they cling to this information and hold it close. Information that does not serve their needs tends to fall away, likely to be remembered and used at a later date when it becomes supportive of a different cause or position in the future.

Achievers love to assess situations and information. They want to know all about the entire situation before they begin taking action because this allows them to operate strategically and efficiently in creating success. One spot where this can become a challenge for them, however, is in the fact that achievers regularly compare themselves to others as a way to measure whether or not they are the best.

This can result in them feeling worse and even struggling to achieve their goals because they are trying too hard to measure up to someone else's success.

When you ask an achiever how they identify themselves, their work that they do tends to be a major part of their identity. It does not matter whether that work is managing a massive corporate company, or stay-at-home parenting, an achiever will excessively identify with the work they do as this is a part of them that can be measured for success. They will often use this as their primary focus for what it is they are trying to achieve in life.

The achiever has feeling patterns that support them in creating success in their life. They are excellent at putting their emotions aside in favor of whatever needs to be done to create success. If their emotions become a problem toward their ability to succeed, the achiever is known to detach from them completely so that they can carry on with success-building actions.

Feelings are one of the harder things for the achiever to face as many believe that they simply get in the way. They are not known to take time aside to reflect on themselves or to invest in processing emotions they face in life. They may throw themselves into a new goal or project to distract themselves from challenging feelings that they are struggling to face. The achiever does not like to ask for help and will often have a hard time reaching out if they do feel they are suffering or struggling with anything.

The achiever wants to look confident and "have the face of success" on at all times. This can result in them putting on a mask over their true feelings. As a result, many achievers have bottled up anger, frustration and sadness that lingers inside of them. This can result in them experiencing anxiety and stress from not expressing it and carrying it around with them. At times, when it becomes too hard to wear the mask anymore, the achiever may completely explode at someone else. They let their temper get the best of them. Then, they put it back away and return to business as usual.

The common blind spots for achievers lie in being able to identify with who they actually are. Because they identify themselves with their success so much, this can result in them having a distorted view of who they are in favor of who they should be. They are extremely conscious of what they look like and how they present themselves, often becoming obsessive about how they look to other people physically and through their self-expression. This can result in them becoming confused and not being able to separate themselves from their work. When this blind spot is particularly pronounced, others may even pick up on this and begin to see the achiever as opportunistic, insincere and ingenuine, and uncaring.

Another major blind spot for the achiever lies in emotions. Often, they don't even realize that they are bypassing challenging emotions and throwing themselves into distracting goals to keep themselves busy. They struggle to face or admit to negative feelings, whether these are their own feelings or someone else's. If someone is giving them negative criticism about something they have done or are doing, they can quickly become defensive and dismissive.

With the achiever being so heavily focused on success, they can quickly become frustrated when other people are not.

This can result in the achiever feeling like they are not being met with the same level of passion in achieving their goals, which can lead to them becoming impatient, frustrated, irritable, and dismissive. They may rush the people around them to get everyone working as efficiently as possible, while failing to realize that not everyone is as success-driven or goal-oriented as they are.

Sometimes, a blind spot that achievers experience is in their confidence being projected as certainty. While certainty is a strong value to have and can be majorly beneficial in various areas in life, it can also seem dismissive from other people. This may end up keeping people avoiding the achiever because they feel their genuine concerns and worries are not understood or valued, which can be uncomfortable for anyone. This can result in people not being as willing to support the achiever in achieving their goals, even if they are supposed to be on the same page – such as in a work setting.

The best way for achievers to begin practicing self-awareness is through paying attention to where they may be dismissing other people and any level of feelings in their life.

They should also take the time to begin recognizing where they may be losing their own identity in favor of the identity they carry with their work. Beginning to recognize where these tendencies arise in their life is a great opportunity for the achiever to begin practicing self-awareness around these tendencies.

Growth Potential

The first and perhaps most obvious point for an achiever to focus on growth lies in learning to identify themselves outside of their work. Realizing that you are not valued or identified by your achievements means that you give yourself the opportunity to know who you truly are. Spend some time understanding and recognizing the difference between who you *are* and what you *do*. Despite what you may have been telling yourself, there is a difference!

It is important to understand that not everyone is going to be motivated in the same way as you are. While it can be easy for you to become frustrated over other people not being as passionate or devoted as you are, it does not serve you as well. A better solution is to recognize this and realize that it is a finite truth. Nothing can change this. You will certainly come across other achievers in life who are like you, but do not do yourself the disservice of believing that all people will be achievers. Instead, pay attention to your communication and work on building communication skills. This way, you can effectively share what needs to be shared with the people involved in reaching your goals without becoming frustrated or upset with them. Learn to motivate people in their own unique ways alongside their own unique needs and it will become a lot easier to lead them to support you in your goals. This is particularly important for achievers in leadership roles who need to enroll a team of people in a mutual vision and encourage all parts of the team to achieve this vision.

Lastly, ensure that you are not dismissive of other people. Take the time to genuinely listen, and understand that your confidence in yourself and your beliefs and opinions does not mean that others cannot experience the same confidence in their own. Giving people a voice and honoring their right to their opinions and beliefs will make it a lot easier for you to maintain positive relationships without being perceived as snooty or rude.

Chapter 24: The Individualist

The individualist personality type is known to be motivated by their need to express their authentic self through their uniqueness. Feelings, purpose, and self-expression are highly valued by the individualist. Of all the personality types, the individualist tends to be among the biggest romantics at heart. They love the beauty of life and love to create meaning in their own life and in the lives of others.

Things to Become Aware Of

When the individualist is balanced, they are sensitive but still very content. In other words, they feel a wide array of emotions but are not typically burdened by them. Their uniqueness and authenticity is the gift they offer to the world, which is typically a radically magnificent gift. They love to work through expression and are commonly known to be artists on some level. Incorporating creativity and meaning into their life gives them great joy.

When they are not balanced, the individualist can become broody. They tend to feel misunderstood and can be experienced by others as temperamental and depressed.

This expression typically arises from their acute awareness of their many wounds and it can lead to them feeling down and frustrated.

The gifts of the individualist include traits such as: self-awareness, purpose-driven, inspiration, sensitivity, and courage. They are highly aware of their own emotions and spend a great deal of their lives trying to understand these emotions and make sense of them. As a result, they are excellent at deeply connecting with others. This also makes them sensitive toward other people and the emotions of those in their lives.

The individualist is driven by the desire of living a purposeful life. They seek activities that contribute to their purpose. They are highly inspired and love to create things from this space of inspiration. The things that they do create are absolutely magical. The individualist is courageous and this helps them in fulfilling and creating their purpose without concern for what other's think or say about what they are doing. Their sense of right versus wrong typically stems from within and what *feels* right versus wrong over anything else.

Due to their emotional connectedness, the feeling patterns of the individualist are very intense. They can feel into the emotions of themselves and their environment easily, allowing them to be very aware of the feelings going on around them. Individualists are known to dwell, often holding onto intense emotions for quite some time. This can lead to them being perceived as moody and intense. Typically, this pattern arises from their desire to feel and understand what their emotions are all about to begin with.

Individualists actually love exploring the emotional spectrum, often moving through emotions as their world changes around them. They deeply resonate with melancholic emotions, leading them often to experiencing cycles of depression. Individualists take life seriously, sometimes too seriously. This can lead to even more melancholy and moodiness. It is important that individualists take the time to explore the more light-hearted emotions as well.

The action patterns typically experienced by the individualist are rooted in their desire to create and experience meaning in their lives. They regularly take action in search of inspiration, meaning, and symbolism. Their artistic expression regularly plays a large role in their ability to create deep and strong relationships with other people. They prefer to spend time with other individualists, as these tend to be the only ones who truly understand the deep emotions and feelings that they have.

Individualists love sharing conversations with other people. Their conversation is generally centered on themselves. They share stories about themselves and generally embellish their stories with artistic creation, using words to help center their listeners into the story as well. They love to use an expansive vocabulary and describe things in the most accurate way possible.

The thinking patterns that individualists experience are generally filled with absence and sensations of envy. They like to focus on what is missing from their lives or from themselves and spend time longing for it. The individualist is incredible at internalizing negative information and developing beliefs about themselves that are rooted in negativity. When positive compliments or information is given to them, the individualist will generally dismiss it and refuses to internalize it.

Something the individualist is well known for is perceiving information and experiences through an emotional lens. They tend to be biased about what information they are interested in and what information they store based on what their emotions declare is good or bad. Even with a pile of facts, the individualist will likely trust their own intuition more than anything else.

The blind spots that the individualist most commonly face are largely based on emotion. For example, individualists long to have deep and meaningful relationships with other people, but regularly dismiss the other person in favor of their own need to be seen as unique and different. This can make it challenging for them to create truly deep and meaningful relationships as it often results in them pushing people away. They also tend to be very centered on themselves, often without realizing how much they are doing it. This can result in other people feeling like they are self-absorbed and perhaps even arrogant.

Another major blind spot that an individualist may experience is their chronic feelings of insufficiency. They tend to hold onto many self-fulfilling prophecies that there is not enough for them, that they are lacking, or that they will never get to experience certain things in life. They can also be dramatic and intense as a result of how they hold onto emotions, including the emotions of others.

The best thing an individualist can do is pay attention to how they may be coming off as self-absorbed and how they can begin to contribute more to the relationships they are in. Through realizing that these blind spots exist and their natural tendencies, individualists can begin to create more deep and meaningful relationships in their lives that are lasting and can serve both parties.

Growth Potential

As an individualist, one of the best areas you can focus on is yourself. Pay attention to your tendency to be focused on yourself and spend some time practicing being genuinely interested in other people. This will help your relationships flourish and will ensure that the other party in your relationship feels honored and cherished as well. Balance your opportunities to talk about yourself with opportunities to talk about the other person and watch how much more people open up to you!

Also, focus on your emotional self. Living a melancholic life may be something you can justify, but it doesn't mean it is going to be the one that brings you the most joy. Instead, it may lead to you experiencing self-fulfilling prophecies that result in you falling into dramatic or melancholic emotional cycles. When you learn how to balance your emotions and take responsibility for your own happiness through action and intention, you can open yourself up for the opportunity to fulfill that which you have been longing for all along.

Chapter 25: The Investigator

Investigators are motivated by their need to understand and know. They value and cherish their ability to learn more and know about the world around them. They are known to be objective and deeply passionate about knowledge and learning. The investigator wants to live a life that is relatively private, often choosing to conserve their resources so that they can remain independent in the future, which is something that they deem as extremely important.

Things to Become Aware Of

When they are balanced, an investigator is known to be mindful and a visionary. They are excellent at remaining unattached from the world around them and offering objective perspectives and viewpoints on the information they have.

When they are not balanced, an investigator can become cheap and stingy with their resources. They can become arrogant on an intellectual level, rejecting other people's information in favor of their own. The investigator can become disconnected from their heart, regularly living from their mind and thoughts rather than from their emotions or from a balance between the two.

Investigators carry the gifts of being perceptive, curious, unsentimental, self-sufficient, and inventive. They are known to carry insightful observations of the world around them, as well as various situations and any data they may come across. Due to their desire to know and learn, they tend to be very curious and will research and explore things that they are drawn to. They love to be independent and are excellent at putting their emotions aside when needed and remaining self-sufficient. They can use their knowledge to create unconventional solutions to the problems they face in life.

When it comes to activity, the investigator is rarely bored. They love spending time alone and are great at coming up with things to do and always keeping themselves busy. They like to build up their resources, recharge, and set clear boundaries and limits. The investigator is passionate about learning activities to help them maintain their independence, as they prefer to have minimal people in their lives and do not like to depend on others.

Due to their desire to scale down, many investigators are known to live a rather minimalistic, frugal lifestyle. Alternatively, they may become hoarders as they will hoard anything that strikes their interest or increases their knowledge.

The investigator's thinking patterns are rooted in knowledge. They live by the motto that knowledge is power and spend their lives consuming all that they can to expand their understanding of various information. They spend a significant amount of their time building expertise and spending time around other individuals who will either help them expand their knowledge, or who are willing to listen and be taught by them.

Given their nature, the investigator is incredible at categorizing information in their mind. They retain information for use at a later date and tend to be the one with the answers to all of life's obvious and not so obvious questions.

When it comes to feelings, the investigator is aligned with that of an introvert. They trust their mind more than their heart and tend to use logical thinking to make decisions, as opposed to paying attention to their feelings. In many instances, they will detach from their feelings completely to make the logical solution happen.

The investigator can be easily emotionally drained, especially if they are spending time in intense or busy situations. They rarely realize that they are emotionally detaching when they do, which can result in them seeming distant and emotionally unavailable to those around them. They would rather take control of their emotions through logic than feel their emotions. The habitual and automatic detachment is a form of self-protection that they use to preserve their energy, once again with the intention of remaining independent.

The blind spots experienced by the investigator often comes from their detachment and their tendency toward being an introvert. Some investigators will struggle to form deep, meaningful relationships with the people in their lives because they quickly detach any time the emotions become intense or challenging. They may also come across as harsh or patronizing in how they share information with people, which is not censored in their personal relationships. This can lead to people feeling as though they are being talked down to, which can further damage the relationships in the investigator's life.

Commitment is not something that an investigator can do with ease. Their desire to remain independent and to keep their circle small can make it challenging for them to maintain relationships. They also tend to be very protective over their resources and their time, which can leave the investigator's friends feeling like the investigator is being stingy toward them. They often struggle to find a balance between helping others feel supported and cared for in relationships.

Growth Potential

As an investigator, your growth potential lies in learning how to be more generous with your time and resources without leaving yourself feeling drained and overwhelmed. The best way to do this is to begin focusing in ways that you can become more involved in relationships while showing care and concern for the other person. There are many ways that you can do this. This will not only help improve your relationships, but it will also help you grow as a person and live a balanced life as well.

The first step is to ensure that you are mindful about how you are sharing with other people. When you are talking to them, pay attention to your tone. If you are sharing information, focus on sharing in a way that teaches the other person. You want to focus on helping them feel engaged, rather than just reciting a bunch of information to them. This will help you be better received by others, making it easier for you to engage in longer conversations that are enjoyable for both parties.

It is also important that you consider your tendency to hoard time, resources, and potentially items. Pay attention to where this motivation comes from, and understand that you can be generous without draining yourself. You can still enjoy your alone time and feel recharged while also having relationships with other people. Allowing yourself to enhance and develop these relationships will help you feel more supported by others which, whether you realize it or not, is an important thing to have in your life.

Learning to balance your emotions and thinking will also be powerful in helping you have better experiences in life. This means that you can still use your logic-based solutions, but you should also take a moment to check in with your emotions to see how they are doing. Facing them and realizing them will ensure that you do not detach and operate in a way that results in you feeling so emotionally drained. When you are aware of how you are feeling and act with these feelings in mind, it becomes easier to preserve your emotional energy on the go and feel more balanced in both independent and group-based settings.

Chapter 26: The Loyalist

The loyalist is motivated by their need to be prepared and safe in any situation and as such, they value belonging and security. They hold trust and loyalty as two highly important traits to have in their lives and in the relationships that they share with other people. They prefer to ensure that they are responsible and want to be prepared for everything at all times.

Things to Become Aware Of

When the loyalist is balanced, they are known to be courageous and connected to their inner knowingness. They are excellent at gifting people with devotion and are known to be deeply trustworthy in themselves and the world around them.

When they are not balanced, the loyalist tends to worry, experience anxiety, and keep walls up against other people. They fear letting anyone in and struggle to trust that they will be kept safe and protected. The loyalist is known to become skeptical and doubtful when they are out of balance.

The gifts that the loyalist possess include devotion, courage, preparedness, trustworthiness, and being team-oriented. They are known to stay committed to their values and the people they value as well.

The typical action patterns experienced by the loyalist is actually split in two different likely patterns. When the loyalist is living with the phobic action pattern, they are known to be very guarded towards people and circumstances. They are very hesitant about taking action or doing anything that could risk their security.

The other way the action pattern might manifest is when they're counter-phobic. This means they try to face things head-on; no matter how much fear is produced by whatever it is they are trying to face. Essentially, they usually exist somewhere between the flight and fight mode and all of their actions come from this space.

When it comes to their thinking patterns, the loyalist is known to avoid problems. They would rather not face them or have to find a solution, so instead, they avoid them. Typically, they try and analyze everything and prepare themselves as much as possible so that no conflict is actually experienced. When this fails, they will typically choose the flight response and flee the situation. They may find distractions or sit in intense anxiety as they attempt to understand why their preparedness was not enough.

In regards to other people, loyalists often think in a way that favors their safety. They may let people in and have thriving relationships, but they also ensure that they never fully let their guards down. This is to avoid being hurt or let down by anyone in their life.

Their feeling patterns are often mixed with anxiety. Nearly all loyalists experience varying degrees of anxiety on a daily basis. This comes from trying to control situations and realizing and regularly manifesting the reality that one simply cannot be in control of and prepared for everything in life.

The blind spots often faced by loyalists are rooted in their need to be prepared for everything. Their intense need to predict everything that could go wrong and then prepare for it to go wrong can come across as stubbornness and pessimism to other people. This can result in them being dismissed or brushed off because others may become overwhelmed or stressed by hearing about all of the ways something could go wrong. This then fulfills the belief that loyalist has, that people are not trustworthy, which further perpetuates that pattern.

Even though the loyalist is devoted to loyal and trust, they are deeply skeptical and doubtful. In many cases, they know that *they* are loyal and trustworthy, and fear that other people will not rise up to meet them with the same devotion. This can result in feelings of unfulfillment, fear in relationships, and an unwillingness to open up to other people.

Growth Potential

The biggest area where loyalists can focus their growth on is in letting their guards down and learning to trust other people. This comes from having true, deep trust for themselves. If you notice that you carry that pattern that includes skepticism and doubt towards other people in your life, begin by focusing on your trust within yourself.

When you can trust your own ability to take care of yourself in any situation, even unexpected ones, it becomes easier to let other people in and experience trust in your relationships. A lot of this comes from reframing where the trust lies. When you try and instill complete trust in someone else, that can feel scary for you. However, when you trust your relationship with someone else and your ability to take care of yourself no matter what, it becomes easier to open up.

Also, ensure that you take time to analyze what could go *right* as well. Getting stuck in analysis paralysis and fear of taking action because you are so focused on all that could go wrong only cements in the fact that things *will* go wrong and you will feel let down as a result. This is because you predicted it would happen, since you predicted every possible thing that could happen. It results in more anxiety and stress, which can lead to you living in a chronic unbalanced state.

Chapter 27: The Enthusiast

The enthusiast is motivated by their desire to experience the best, most enjoyable life possible. They are also motivated by avoiding experiencing pain. Enthusiasts value freedom, optimism, inspiration, opportunity, and enjoyment. They like to see life as an adventure filled with much potential and desire to experience as much of the adventure as possible.

Things to Become Aware Of

When the enthusiast is living in a balanced state, they are content and serene. They embrace sobriety and enjoy a deep sense of presence. They are excellent at rooting themselves in the moment, enjoying both themselves and the world around them.

When they are not balanced, the enthusiast is known to be impulsive, unfocused, uncommitted, and distracted. They become afraid of missing out and therefore chase any opportunity to experience joy that they can find. This can result in them feeling unfulfilled and struggling to find any sense of fulfillment in anything they do.

The gifts of the enthusiast include being optimistic, flexible, future-oriented, practical and adventurous. They love having fun and choose to see life through rose-colored glasses. They are always looking forward to the bigger picture and, when they're balanced, they are particularly skilled at bringing any vision to life.

The enthusiast is typically dominant in their thinking patterns. They are known to have a highly active mind that is continually moving through thoughts and emotions. They have a really high need for mental stimulation and can become easily bored. The enthusiast is a great storyteller and is incredible at exercising their imagination. They are known to be extremely creative as a result of their imagination. The enthusiast wants to be aware of all of the choices and options available to them as this helps them access the opportunity and adventure that life has to offer.

Because the enthusiast can become bored quickly, their actions are often rooted in thrill-seeking. They do not like doing anything repetitive or tedious, this can actually result in them feeling depressed or stressed. Instead, they prefer to have momentum in life and move forward with great joy and motivation. They are known to have a busy body language due to their excessive energy, and are often restless.

Enthusiasts always want to feel good and regularly look to create and fulfill positive emotions. They love joy, optimism and enthusiasm. They get very uncomfortable around negative emotions such as fear, anxiety, and boredom. They always instinctively work toward feeling happy and will regularly use planning for the future as a way to escape current feelings of dissatisfaction or sadness.

They do not like to be questioned in their ability. Enthusiasts are easily upset when people do not believe in them and their abilities. They prefer to be surrounded by others with the same optimistic and opportunistic style as they are.

The common blind spots for enthusiasts comes around their high energy. They often want to be the master but rarely have the desire to devote to learning so that they can actually become the master. Instead, they would rather become an "instant expert" and may end up only having half of the knowledge that is actually available to them.

The communication style of the enthusiast is very bold and expressive, especially in their body. To them this is how they embody their high energy, but to others it can become distracting and even frustrating. Because it is so stimulating, it may completely turn off others with different personality types that are more calm and collected.

Enthusiasts are masters at assuming. They have a quick mind and love to assume that they know what the other person is going to say or do. This results in them often assuming wrong and this can easily lead to problems.

Lastly, the enthusiast does want to be fully accepting of themselves but is rarely still enough to do so. They often struggle to commit to the activities that will enable them to be this way. They rationalize mistakes they have made and rush out of feelings of sadness or otherwise "down" emotions to get back into their feel-good state. This can result in them running away from their problems and never fully embracing what needs to happen for them to truly accept themselves.

Growth Potential

The best opportunity for an enthusiast to grow lies in slowing down and actually experiencing life as it is happening. When they are balanced, the enthusiast is highly present. This ensures that they are available to experience the wide range of emotions and that they actually work through the ones they experience. In doing so, they heal a lot more of their chronic life stories and are able to access their highest expression of happiness and joy.

As an enthusiast, you also need to be mindful that most people are not as energetic or spontaneous as you are. This can become frustrating for both of you, as you are easily bored and need stimulation, and many other personality types are easily over stimulated and need to slow down. Taking the time to understand this and honoring the other person's needs is a great way to ensure that you are keeping your relationships healthy and are not putting excessive pressure on yourself or anyone else.

Chapter 28: The Challenger

The challenger is motivated by their need to be strong. They are also motivated by ensuring that no one sees them as vulnerable or weak. Challengers value their control and are excellent at being impactful and direct in their approach.

Things to Become Aware Of

When they are balanced, the challenger is known to be deeply caring, strong, and supportive to others. They are protective and often seen as a gentle leader.

When they are not balanced, the challenger can become domineering, lustful, and aggressive. This is how they attempt to make themselves look tougher so that they can hide their true vulnerability.

The gifts possessed by the challenger include being assertive, decisive, protective, independent and influential. They make for great leaders and, when balanced, tend to lead from a very down-to-earth perspective. They care for everyone that they are leading and for everyone in their life.

However, they are still effective in caring without compromising their own well-being.

The action patterns regularly experienced by the challenger includes things like acting on instinct. They tend to be very instinct-based and are able to operate like this as though it is their second nature. When their instinct tells them one way or another, they listen and they make whatever needs to happen, happen.

They can be very direct and intense, and typically keep their body language monitored to ensure that they are expressing strength and toughness in their body language as well. They pride themselves on being in control of everything, from their physical actions to their thoughts and emotions. This is how they show strength.

Challengers typical thought patterns are rooted in judging things and people as either weak or strong. They will then treat the other person or situation based on how they have judged it. They tend to have a very all-or-nothing approach to things in their life.

A challenger despises investing too much time thinking about small details and prefers to look at, and work toward, the bigger picture. They don't respond well to charm, force, or bribery. If they see something as unimportant or they simply don't want to do it, these tactics will not encourage them to take action.

The feeling patterns experienced by the challenger are generally based on anger. They are quick to get angry and they often use this anger as fuel to get them into immediate action. They move on quickly and avoid any emotions that make them appear weak or vulnerable, such as sadness.

Challengers are rarely aware of how intimidating they can come across to others, which tends to be a major blind spot for them. As a result, those that they intimidate are often seen as weak and, therefore, are warranted little respect, admiration, appreciation or attention from the challenger.

Their unwillingness to be vulnerable can often lead to challengers being seen as emotionally unavailable and too "hard" in relationships. They struggle to open up to others and to be fully expressed. This can lead to the people with whom they share relationships feeling neglected, uncared for, or unappreciated. This is not because the challenger does not actually care, but because the way they show their care and emotions is quite different from how people tend to be receptive of it.

Growth Potential

The best opportunities for growth for a challenger include learning how to find comfort in being vulnerable. This does not mean that you need to let your guard down and let everyone in, but knowing how to express "weak" emotions comfortably can have a powerful impact on your ability to move forward. It is actually a mark of strength, not weakness.

You should also take time to learn to slow down and think more rationally in your life. Although working on instinct is a valuable trait, taking the time to actually think through situations can be extremely helpful in ensuring that you are not quick to jump into action without knowing the full story.

Chapter 29: The Peacemaker

The peacemaker is motivated by their need to be harmonized with the world and settled in life. They value peace and stability and tend to avoid conflict.

Things to Become Aware Of

When they are balanced, the peacemaker is known to be self-aware and vibrant. They are able to harmonize the world around them and bring peace and calmness to every situation they are in.

When they are not balanced, the peacemaker can become stubborn, self-denying, and procrastinating. This stems from trying to perpetuate a false sense of peace in an otherwise uncomfortable situation.

The gifts of the peacemaker include being agreeable, understanding, patient, supportive and genuine. They tend to be extremely easy to get along with and are able to understand multiple different perspectives. They are excellent at finding something in common with virtually everyone.

The general action patterns expressed by the peacemaker are rooted in their inner conflict. They regularly want to control their environments, but do so in a way that is very passive. They avoid conflict at all costs and, when it does arise, they use passive strategies to stop it. The peacemaker tries to balance the energies and personalities of all of the individuals in the room, and likes to experience harmony with everyone.

Peacemakers use their thinking patterns to produce structured processes, attention to detail, and clarity. They love habits and are able to produce new ones quickly and easily. They also tend to be great at organizing information and details easily, no matter how many there are. To the people who do not truly know the peacemaker, they may not realize that they are actually incredibly stubborn.

The feelings of the peacemaker tend to be extremely intense. They are known to be even-tempered and easy-going to others, but inside they often experience many vibrant emotions, and they do so in a deep and intense way. They like to keep these strong and intense feelings to themselves to refrain from having conflict with other people. It is easier for the peacemakers to keep these feelings to themselves in favor of harmony.

One major blind spot that peacemakers experience is in their passive behavior. Since they avoid being controlled but try to control others, which results to intense passive aggression. As a result, they can directly impact their relationships with this indirect action.

Because of their need to have everyone harmonized, peacemakers are known to explore multiple perspectives and then try to share these with everyone. This can often lead to long, drawn out explanations of various topics, resulting in people not listening. This can be disheartening for the peacemaker, leading to feelings of rejection. Since rejection is a conflict-based feeling in the minds of the peacemakers, they will likely internalize that and not truly face it later on.

Growth Potential

The biggest opportunity for a peacemaker to experience growth is in learning to be assertive and have boundaries. Recognizing how to embrace and use conflict in a positive way, rather than it automatically being assumed to be an act of anger or aggression can help peacemakers express themselves in a more powerful way. This ensures that your needs are being met and that you are not bottling things up, but also that you are able to stay more in alignment with your desire for harmony.

It is also important that you learn that not everyone is as motivated by peacemaking as you are. As such, not everyone is going to be as calm and collected as you are, or as you come across. Learning to honor people is a great way to ensure that you are keeping the peace in a way that is productive and that does not involve you taking control over everyone and becoming passive aggressive.

Communication is the biggest area in which you need to focus your attention on. Learning to communicate powerfully, intentionally, and with purpose and directness will ensure that you are understood and received in the best way possible.

Conclusion

The Enneagram is an incredible tool that gives you the opportunity to know yourself better. When you take the test and discover what you are driven by, it becomes easier to understand who you are and why you behave the way you do. Furthermore, it shines a light on areas of yourself where improvement can be made so that you can live in the balanced expression of yourself and honor your highest good and the highest good of all.

I hope this book provided you with all that you were looking for in terms of discovering what an Enneagram is and how this incredible personality test can help you grow as a person and experience deeper success in your relationships.

The next step is to begin practicing and exercising self-awareness based on your personality type and subtype. Then, you can begin looking for opportunities to bring yourself into alignment with the positive expression of your type. This will support you in further bettering yourself, your relationships, and expressing your personality in a more aligned way.

Lastly, if you enjoyed reading this book and felt that it added value to your life, I ask that you please take a moment to review it on Amazon Kindle. Your honest feedback would be greatly appreciated.

Thank you.

Printed in Great Britain
by Amazon